CW01657642

MissyMoo ©

ISBN 978-0-6399437-6-3

5% of all profits from the sale of this book will be donated to

help2read
improving lives through literacy

Registered Non-Profit 063-979

PBO 930027054

UK Charity Reg No. 1109567

Dedicated to all those affected by the 2018 volcanic eruptions in Hawaii

20% of profits from the sale of this book will be donated to The Hawaii Island Volcano Recovery Fund established by The Hawaii Community Foundation, to assist with recovery efforts in support of Hawaii Island communities affected by the Kilauea volcano eruption.

Missymoo is just like you. She's smart and pretty and funny.

She goes to school like good girls do and loves her little pet bunny!

She's flying high up in the sky with her entire family.

Missymoo, her folks and brother Jake are on their way to Hawaii.

A group of islands off the U.S mainland, located in the Central Pacific.

With volcanoes and waterfalls and mountains so tall. Hawaii really sounds terrific!

CANADA
U.S.A
JAPAN
HONOLULU
MEXICO
HAWAII
PAPUA NEW GUINEA
PACIFIC OCEAN
AUSTRALIA
NEW ZEALAND

As a matter of fact, to be more exact, they're going to

Honolulu.

They've been counting the sleeps forever and ever, but hey, wouldn't you too?

After a very long flight, all through the night, they arrive at their hotel.

They are given a Lei and shown the way by a lovely young lady named Belle.

Belle

First things first, what should they do? They suggest one thing each.

"*Shopping*" says Mum, "*Hiking*" says Dad. Missy and Jake say "*The Beach!*"

THE BEACH

Try as they might, Mum and Dad lose the fight. It’s off to the beach they go!

Flip flops and hats, buckets and beach mats...and sun cream for a nice healthy glow.

Whenever they travel, this family likes to dabble in as much local culture as possible.

They stay away from the malls and eat at local food stalls. It's what makes a holiday phenomenal!

ALOHA Juice Bar
FRESH COCONUT JUICE $2

They are on their way now to a special Lu'au for all the hotel guests.

Missymoo is asked to join the Hula dance. She has so much fun and does her best.

So next time you're asked to try a new task, just remember this one special thing.

Even though you may be wary, or it might seem scary, who knows what magic it will bring!

BE BRAVE

27882596R00016

Printed in Poland
by Amazon Fulfillment
Poland Sp. z o.o., Wrocław